MW00610762

Timeless Resonance

To George my
"sliding" teacher,
whos magic
embraced my
tango...
Happy Birthday
Happy retirement!
♡♡
Jane

Timeless Resonance

A POETIC ADVENTURE TO HIGHER CONSCIOUSNESS

Jana Liba Klenburg

LONE PINE PRESS
NEW YORK

First Edition 1996
All rights reserved

Copyright by Jana L. Klenburg
© 1996

Library of Congress
CIP
Catalog-Card-Number: 96-78509

Published by Lone Pine Press,
an imprint of:

Global Book Productions, Incorporated
23 West 35th Street
New York, NY 10001

ISBN #0-9632920-4-8

Printed in the United States of America on
Acid-free paper

---

10 9 8 7 6 5 4 3 2 1

To my wise and beautiful children
my teachers

Dimitry Boss
Ilana Boss Markowitz

I ACKNOWLEDGE

My loving family, beloved friends--you all
know who you are, for allowing me to
become through your love.
Roberto for the children.
Pepe, for your unwavering acceptance.
The Blessed memory of my Rabbi,
Reb Shlomo Carlebach.
"A Course in Miracles," whose teachings
saved my life.
Neil, for being yourself and making my
daughter happy.
My wise and generous editor, Louise Temple
Barrett .

Cover: Illustration "Angel and Sun meet Earth,"
Jana Klenburg '93.
Graphic design and calligraphy,
Anthony Bloch.

TABLE OF CONTENTS

Love Poems

THE MERENGE KING

Dancing to the beat of sweat and strobe
swirling into magic
your hands treasure my body
clothed in silk and translucent glitter,
wrapping your heat around me
in the ballroom of romance,
    entrancing rhythm
the merenge pulses
sweeping up stars and moon in dance,
we are breathing in Spanish
Llevameee... que me muero por besar tu piel...
llevameee... aventurera...[1]
we are one flow
a zenith of bodies where all reason is void.

Drenched
you hold my hand on your heart as we dance
flooding me in your sea,
I hold your body with my body
surrendering, impassioned, my sweat to you
and in an inner dance of light and shadow
we become the rhythm of each other's freedom.

Stars explode in my brain

We are barely lace
made of silken thread and timeless tastes.
Spinning me with your will above ground
you become a summer storm that carries me
and I rain throwing itself to your wind.

Kamasutra[2] wizard, elegant dancer, astral propeller
you rocket us together into the void
where our bodies knowing
beyond reason, beyond past
make now happen in a trance:
a mating of thunder.

When the sun has barely awakened
and the passion-nightclub closes
we say goodbye on the street,
and as we walk away from each other
our shadows stretch behind us
meeting
in a passionate lengthy kiss.

---

1. Take me...that I'm dying to kiss your skin...take
me...adventuress...

2. Sanskrit treatise setting forth rules for love and marriage.
Also a manual of sexual behavior.

OUR "BEGIN THE BEGUINE"

In God I trust
for the humbleness to love you,
to conquer myself
in the freshness of the gift
that is you. I've waited
for the time when your eyes
no longer change
between the intimate and the mundane,
the day my hair is your laughter
and your softness my trust

In the gift that you offer
we are healed

Tonight you grace my tired room
with a smell of honey
and your fragrant touch.
We have begun the dance of our
    "Begin,
        Do
           Begin"

I need you in the freedom of us
and kiss the leftover stars
in the curls below your waist,
a silent synchronicity ignites
and my center opens
like a lotus in a lake

You take me in your arms of earth
and I envelope you so gently in mine
there is no pain and no fear
just one breath of oh, such sweet flight,
and in our alchemized flow
sailing the moment—
the perfect compromise between life and death—
we enter the ancient ritual of surrender
our breath knowing no time
I swallow your sea

At dawn
still languishing in our rapture
I pray to be worthy of your love.

THE ZEN OF NO TOUCH

In the sanctuary of passion
you dazzle my depth.
Your married man's eyes
blue and wanting
echo my inner shrine

You slide through my skin
light upon light
without touching
and know my secrets
before you hear

My Zen of knowing...
Your Zen of commitment...
guide us in grace

Our bodies don't meet
and we touch only God

PABLO, MAESTRO!

Neruda
justice is your breath
fearless in knowing
tattooed by the wind
love carved in faith
the poet of poets
your song completed the world

I began with the best
you were the first.
At eleven I found
"Twenty Love Poems
and One Song Of Despair."
Transmuted by the thoughts you think
with the feelings I felt
I came to be
in flight with your flight
a peace making song of grapes

Noble man of Nobel Prize
Chilean forever
embracing your wounded land
fixing its broken mouth
tending its tragic de-petalled daisies

You inhabit me
afire
your words dialogue
with my inner wisdom
you know of distant sadness
and in your voice that has humbled itself
into a homeless poem of exile
a searing truth lives where God flames.
Justice finds its place in your hand.
With each of your words we breathe in freedom
and breathe out pain

I was twenty one when
at the New York Hilton
we met in a strange cadence
of slow motion.
Your wife, Matilde, in the background
looked on accustomed to the routine
as I sat beguiled at your feet
amongst many others,
and in my wiser years as a poet
I've continued at your feet
still translating into Nerudian
when I don't want facts
to interfere with truth

Last night, Pablo maestro,
I slept in the same dream as you
a merciful atonement
of making love in a quiet poem
where in each other's exiles
we to one another sang

When you were dying
your forever betraying government
cut off your phone from all the world,
as the wood fences around your homes
bore the packed, scratched tributes
from the humble for whom you sang
to the famous that sang for you

This is a small "song of despair"
as I wash my face with your tears
I again know your rhymes
visionary of hot rhythms
your drum is my heart beat
and your voice is my song!

TESTOSTERONE FOG

So I gave in and made sex
risking the grace of the enduring dance
that perhaps could have been.
Your deep want
throughout two full moons
dowsed my aloneness,
so I gave in and made sex.
My exuberance didn't warn you
to be sensitive...
and to keep your heart
where your body was

Astonished at your abandonment
I watched you
from outside myself
confusing experience with truth
in a solitude of passion

And now, how do we follow this act?

YOUR BREATH INTO MY BREATH

In the sanctuary of night
your hands entangle

Your breath
into my breath
mine
to breathe

I move
gently
into your surf
willing it as my own
and sing
hoarsely
within your hair
wild
and soft
over my waters

And we dissolve
into each other
in a boundless glow of
oh, so brief a surrender
in a wave of timeless moistures
and the light of one desire.

PERSONALS

From my outrageously expensive newspaper ad
to only one answer I replied.
In subsequent letters he was perfectly "new age"
which I so deeply crave.

He travelled three hours for us to meet

As I open the door
my breath takes a leap.
He for sure looks the part, that he does!
Salt and blond longish hair
slender and strong, artistically clothed
blues that see deep and far
just as he had described.

Eleven hours we spent on that day

Quietly
zen-like by my window
facing the Hudson
he says: "I think you know
how much knowing you
has begun to mean—
we are old souls."
Perfectly new age he is
speaks the part
looks the part, oh yes he does!
Everything is cautioning me, he will
walk on my soul, neurologically
mug my sweet brain, massacre
the honored place in my self with
his almost elegant remoteness...

The ancient longing to be loved
takes over the child within me
I'll give this a chance,
he feels what I feel...
looking deep into me
he murmurs
"when I see you I see pure light...
it's like I've known you forever..."
my anxious heart
mired in nostalgia
jumps
into the grip of "forever,"
a magical coincidence of oneness...

He must have an empty house
in his refrigerator, I think
feeling the chill again
in learning he has rare contact
with his six children
from two different wives.

Looking around with his architect's sense
he says: "Your home
is magnificent...I love your art,
your pottery, all that you make
is your inner shrine."—
Oh God, same words that I use—
my home...my inner shrine
I'm swept away again, sucked in, overtaken
...*i otra palabra que no puedo recordar* [1]
confusing anxiety with ardor.

He moves his hand closer without touching
our brains make love in the sipping of tea
he speaks of
Sheldrake's quantum theory of morphic fields
as if he knew in a place of old
my love for quantum anything...
I gobble up the words
moist between my thighs—
the forever-nostalgia again
an archetype I so readily recognize
Oh! Ying[2] me to the moon! I'm lost!

Oh take me, hold me, contain me
make me yours for ever again!
It's this feeling that is warning me
if he touches me, that's it
I will never be mine.
I close my eyes
without moving my hands
I grasp my heart
experience being split from myself,
out of my body, I watch what is happening...

He is a danger in the world of women,
we are loving in quicksand,
L.S.D. told him of wisdom
but wisdom he doesn't have.

Reborn through you
your essence in me
birth and death all in one
I'm alone once again.

His hand caresses my nape and jump starts my yes!
I feel panicked and aroused
again sexualizing my fear
I clutch my heart harder, a life-saving grip
to cradle my indwelling child
and rescue myself
from becoming flesh of his flesh
from loosing myself in his want
from facing myself through him
from thinking I could find God through a man!

---

1. Spanish for "...and...another word I can't remember."

2. A poetic combination of Yin for feminine and Yang for masculine, the opposing cosmic principles in Chinese philosophy.

VIENNESE WALTZ

...and here we are in love perhaps...
I, in sophisticated matte silk
a fairy tale gown,
on my left wrist, a rose ready to fade
you, in garments of fire and your lengthy green gaze,
my hand in yours, a pale featherless wing
your hand, fragrant heat around my waist,
vigilant, my expectant body
awaits your first move...
the air is palpitating
a dissolution of boundaries about to begin...
the music fills the ballroom like a bonfire
it's the "Anniversary Waltz" ... My mother's favorite!
You fly me within you, whisking us
into a world of perfection
a common language that makes us one,
whirling through centuries
nothing to fear in the crossing of thresholds
dancing ourselves into weightless rapture
a mutuality of blaze.
My volatile hair takes flight
wrapping itself around empty spaces,

and in an act of faith—
as sacred forces mate in limitless space—
I surrender to the whirlwind
in which we love one another in Viennese rhyme,
there, your trustworthy hold
unleashes my rainforest within.

The sweetness of the night
the scent soft as foam knowing no time
delivers me to a childhood wonder
a magical incarnation
in which my dashing father who seemed so tall
swirling me would say, "Float...
raise your left arm
arch your back
float...just float...!"
I feel your leg between mine earthing me now
to release the spin in the opposite direction
where the wind holds its breath
and my glitter shoes sway their happiness...
I am back, here in your arms
embraced in one thousand wrappings

In waltz we are certain... Yes!

TONIGHT I SMELL OF JUNGLE

Like the beginning of a new religion
I wanted our love to be...

This want
born from ancient inner silence
howls
in the wounded night
as I see the snow fall
on the Hudson
this funky Sunday eve

My darling, bring your heart close
for I am cold.
Tonight I smell of jungle
and my trusting raped heart
is wet from hail.

SHIVAH[1]

He died in me
when the flurries
trapped my lungs
on that deaf December dawn.

I sat shivah
for two months and six days,
didn't know he had passed
till the end of that time.

Three days ago
I saw him walking in the street
his long hair wrestling in the gale
his multicolored beard speckled in snow
wearing that elegant raincoat
bought in "Bloomies"
one Thursday afternoon
with much luck.

He sent metal *shalach monos*[2]
and daffodils wrapped in wind
as he prayed and prayed
striving to adapt to this physical world.

I accepted he was gone from my life.
Just six days and two months
after the wintery wake
I'm feeling the pain.

---

1. Traditional seven day mourning period for a relative or a very close person, in which Jews "sit" shivah.

2. Presents of two or more foods exchanged at the Jewish holiday of Purim.

WINE GARDEN

Urged by your weight
wrapped around you
all at once
we become.
The sages of my faith
would consign this passion to night
and here it is now
Sunday afternoon—
your pants
folded by the bedside,
and the light too bright
for the shielding shade
of night

but I just close my eyes
and dance your depth.

THE OTHER WOMAN

At her friend's wedding
sucking in her cheeks
to chisel her face
she invents happiness and bliss
rocked by her sweetheart
adulterer's arms

Clear-sighted, wise
but drowning in her yearning
she believes
he will leave his wife, now of grown kids,
for so he rambled
for a lengthy spell

Sixteen months since yesterday
in his lie
waiting every day
against her wisdom she hopes
in daydream and despair...

THE CELEBRATION THAT IS US

Drench yourself in rain
this morning I want you
bathed in holy waters

In the turbulence of our geographical clash
let us shimmer as we love,
rise into one another
as the awakening day
kiss
and eat our laughter

I've filled our cave
with gentle things
and rinsed your robe
with softener

In the celebration that is us
we are safe
in the strength of our song.

YOU ARE THE LIGHT

You are the light
by which
I see myself

my higher self
my crazy self
the kindest me

the light between
my light and
The Light itself

you are the light
by which
I see myself

I LOVE MAKING LOVE:
THE NEVERLAND OF SURPRISE

I love making love
standing in a hammock
smelling your hair
rubbing my belly to your fragrance
chewing on your nose

I love making love
in the afternoon vehemence
          of Pablos
Picasso's, Neruda's, Casals'
paintings, poetry and who knows what
on their beds of flowers
cellos and chili sauce
oh ma baby don't love me no mo
wo wo wo wo wo

On that mothering chair
making love with your tangerine laughter
endless-slow
ever-now
constant-more
lost in your grapefruit
your mango in my hair.
In the eighteenth century
of your hebrew thighs
my ripening loins
rejoice in your mind...
and we play footsy like the octopus
Oedipuss
puss
oh my I'm running loose...

I love making love
inside out
in your messy room
of London Bridges
falling down,
falling down...

To make love in your room
peeling off your musical socks
and covering up your Holy books.
I love making love
in the honey of your eyes
where your passion consumes
my Mexican genie
and burns the succulent door that
I sealed long ago
waiting for you

To make love in your tofu and noodles
with tamari on top,
to come and come
to your parents' home
Sunday mornings to buy clothes
and tell family tales
of suitcase lives, of
feathery desserts and
opium options
as I pay for the gas in the car
to get there...

I love making love
through your body of light and fire
of nuts and bolts
eating pomegranates
and candied violets arranged
on the lapis lazuli dish

I love making love with relative measure
where three hairs on your head
are too little
and three hairs in your soup
are too much...

I love making love
in the neverland of surprise
and your harsh whispers that whisper
I love you
love you
love
ya
ma baby ma love!

KNOWING YOUR EYES

There is a blaze
somewhere someplace
in my velvet center
I am ablaze

Cherishing your awakening
of craving and pleasure
of soft waters and secrets

A passion-glow
yielding the lava
of surrender

The nectar glow
in knowing your eyes.

PHILADELPHIA HILTON

Your body of light, of air
my body of earth, and fire
make love
on a very wide window sill
ever higher, higher

I love your head
also your crazies
and your African daisy

My brain is yours
our breath is wine

On a window sill ever higher
we adjust our flight
of light and earth
of air and fire

THROUGH YOUR BODY

Through your body
I touch heights
and depths
through your body I touch

Through your body
I lose but to gain
your being in mine
through your body I gain

Through your body
I become in my center
in yours
through your body I become

Through your body
I sing your renewal
in mine
through your body I sing

Through your body I die,
In the welding of love
is the pleasure of God
through your body to God

LOVE IS NOT MADE OF SKINS

How can a very small heart
contain a craving so big?

I have watched my unborn love grow
reaching the speed of blood
in a solitude of passion

And my soulmate
a perpetual dialogue with a ghost.
Did I miss the universal rhyme?

Love is not made of skins

I long for the infinite
the mystery that cannot be spoken
a love that survives the seasons
a moment of instant totality
where gratefulness is the natural way
a pure heavy honey from the center of my juice
a place where one rests from oneself
and for a shimmering moment feels safe
and glows

That craving indeed
is for God, people say...
true
but what do I do with the flesh?

Family Poems

I NEVER KNEW MY GRANDPARENTS

I have this rage that I can never feel.
Bereft of unconditional love
the deepest healing
grandparents that spoil us as we grow
grandparents I never knew
Treblinka
fifty seven aunts and uncles
that have no face
for me
no cousins to play with,
A nazi attempt
to exterminate
the fire of the burning bush.
Six years of no-light days and vacant moons
Treblinka
where the smell of terror is still in the ground
fifty years later.
Of my mother's family, all that remains
are three sepia photographs...
Bubi Chaya[1], Zeide[2] Abraham
I look for your dignified faces,
ingrained in my brain
I look at the newsreels from Poland
where mountains of bodies
still soft of limb
are shoved by mechanical plows
into communal holes
where the earth still moves.
Zeide, where is your magical violin?
Bubi, where is your cholent[3]
your Sabbath stew
"the best that has ever been made"
my mother repeatedly said.

Bubi Zelda, on father's Russian side,
all that is left of your family
only one small photo of you!
I see your peasant stern face
and my heart in exile reaches
for your eyes
that shone with knowing

Tonight I cannot sing.
How can one speak in poems
of missing this never experienced love?
My head hurts so
that I can hear the dust fall

Hitler also had a mother, they say,
who begot a holocaust of one
a genetic nightmare
with a love for music and an iron heart

A holocaust of one
three
fifty-seven
six million it was

Four photos is all I have
and this rage that I can never feel.

---

1. Diminutive for the Jewish word Bube - Grandma

2. Yiddish for Grandpa

3. Traditional stew, kept warm from Friday evening to
Saturday's day, in accordance with the
non-kindling law of the Sabbath.

NATURAL BIRTH

In the zenith of day
you were born
forcefully
trembling in your silver moist light.
Your cry of ocean waves quenched my fear,
and when you finally came into my thirsty arms,
fingers and toes complete,
the perfection of beauty revealed itself
anointing my rapture.

My Dimitry Meir,
your eyes and mine
saw into one another
letting me know early
of your wisdom.
You smiled, for an Angel of Grace
flew above you.

There must surely be a God
for a being like you to exist.

DID IT HAPPEN?

How do I think that I know?
Alone as a child
when I hated my body
and my mind would sweat fear,
when I wanted to die
and realized I already had.
Those sleepless watchful times
when one eye is open
throughout the night,
when awakened
by my heart's own beat ...
Is that how I know?

Alexander,
Tell from the grave

SHE DIED IN MY ARMS JUST LIKE THAT

She died in my arms
just like that.
She relaxed like a child
fluid drained from her nose
she pushed out her denture
and relaxed like a child

Her jet-black and silvery hair
released its sixty eight year glow.
She relaxed like a child,
pale, very pale
and beautiful, so beautiful
in my arms helpless and lost

"Two screams ...
I heard two screams!"
said the nursing-sister
rushing into the room—
"Two children,
she must have had two children,
for I heard only two screams,"
she said...

My aunt Rishka
with her child-like blue eyes
forlorn, just stood there,
her sister, my mother
gone
the last of her family
gone...

My mother surrendered her flesh
to the flesh of her flesh
and I surrendered her body
to linen and legal affairs

My brother
took care of things

I went home for a sheet
to wrap around her

When we came
to my father that midnight
he was sitting in darkness ...
we just embraced
he and my brother shed tears
and in silence
we saw the sun rise

I didn't speak for two days
there was nothing to say

one year later I cried

ON THE DAY I WAS FIVE

I remember the long distance call
from Mexico to the United States
on the day I was five
Aunt Rishka breathed a sigh of relief
handed my father the phone
then I knew Mom hadn't died

When she came back
from the Mayo Clinic again
she once more had a suitcase
      of magic and toys
      soap bubble pipes
      and diamonds you could eat
      as they sparkled in your mouth

In the other suitcase
stained with dry blood
she had bandages and cloths
and weird things I did not understand

She was in bed
when I looked with anxious breath
into her face,
she opened her eyes
winked at me
and gave me a smile.
Being sure she hadn't died
I came back to life
and took a big breath
on the day I was five

WOUNDED PARADOXES

My Father's body is lying in the morgue,
there is a chair waiting nearby
for we Jews watch our dead till burial
so no spirit can trespass the body

The chair is empty,
nobody is keeping vigil!
Should I?

I hesitate for a flash
and run out of the room

Though I'm already a mother
one can be a coward at twenty nine.

MY DAUGHTER, MY CHILD

We finally came to grips with one another
and with our selves
just in time before you moved faraway...

Last night I had a dream, my daughter:
you stood in a garage, cold,
in your thermal long-johns, embracing yourself,
looking forlorn and dismayed
seeing your things being taken away,
I held you tenderly in my arms
and you sobbed and sobbed your pain away...
I woke up startled
holding only myself
and crying out our pain.

ILANA

The week Ilana fought
to return
from the lure of death
all week long
I held her pale, bruised hand
in mine
firm in life
tender and soft

In her swollen, absent face
the black rings
around her eyes
marked her fight
for seven long weeks

In my daughter's innocence
her lost panicked eyes
searched mine
as I looked through hers
seeking God
to keep her—
flesh of my flesh—
in life.

INNOCENCE

3 a.m.: The Steinway
played itself.
Our cat,
I long ago forgot his name,
walked on the keyboard
perhaps to entertain himself
and the souls floating
on that fresh summer night

Mom was scared
Dad was brave
I laughed quietly,
I taught him to do that.

THIS HOLOCAUST OF YOU AND I

A song of rage
and whiplash.

You think
you can still get away with
"I love you forever"
but love you for never.
You are a grown-up. Grow up!
You have my genes,
no longer can your pain use me.
The air is filled with screaming
I am rage
my karate tongue bites itself
as I face myself through you
death sheds darkness
into the collective shadow,
your blindness
awakens echoes of memory wounds
endlessly reiterated
heartless executions.
I stand helpless through empty dawns
swallowing bloodstained tears
as I watch the leaves
consuming the early dew.

I WAS 13 ON THAT DAY

Drowned in anxiety
at my birthday party
amidst a blackout
I sheltered under the table
and remembered the dream:

> There was a sweet child
> in the garbage
> tossed amongst dead chickens and dogs
> her little hand
> shaking hands with the wind
> reaching for someone to grab
> but no one reached back.

Under the table, blackout still on,
she realized
something was dreadfully wrong

She grew
accomplished and celebrated
desired by many men
inventing magic windows
and fantasies of romantic love.

Still forlorn,
with her blond curls
singing in the wind,
all she felt she had
was a questioning mind
a vague craving for God
and a red pain in her heart.

THERE IS ONLY GOD

The heavens rejoice
Yehuda Eli has arrived!

You were given to us
with a grace of presence
an angel's breath
and a luminous body
housing a secret shadow.
Like an eagle of light
you gifted us with the wisdom of old

There is only God

You appeared shimmering
through the pain of the flesh
just as we dreamed you
and beyond
a golden catalyst
the perfect child of God's love

In the quiet turbulence
of your ephemeral life
our eyes met at the start
with a love
that only in the formless endures…
As you slipped further away from our grasp
we kept reaching beyond the reach of flesh
our fingers growing longer
behind your parents' hands
that have almost no fingers left

There is only God

At the end,
with tired breath
your sweet heart struggling to survive,
the peace of your indwelling home
unfolded the mystery to us
of the flow of God's law

There is only God

My God-child
we know how much of you we contain.
When I saw
your colorful animal blanket
covering the tiny bundle of your body
on top of ice
the size of you
slapped me to reality
and your whisper resonated in my bones

From dust to dust
My chaotic rage burns.
I do not understand!

There is only God

A song of silence.
Nothing that I can say will be enough.
We have come undone and we stand
with empty greedy passion
sobbing orphans of love

Formless and free
You have become a prayer

Now my Angel of Light
embraced by your parents' faith
your little brother's longing
and the love of us all,
you can live your dream safely
within the source of Mercy
where our Rebbe[1] sings!

Yisgadal, Viyiskadash[2] ...

---

1. Endearing term for Rabbi.

2. Exalted and Sanctified... the first words from
the Kaddish, the Jewish mourner's prayer.

Spiritual Poems

OH LORD, INSPIRE

To channel an ode
in consensual flight
with the All
where loving now
is not in fear of tomorrow
where reincarnational fatigue is no more,
seducing myself
into sanity
ad infinitum

Sparkler of my blue roses
inspire
end these delusional cardiac arrests
plumb more peaceful nights
and help us to play
with our chakras[1] at dawn

Oh Lord
my beginning and my end
...and with luck
        my middle too ...!
inspire me
to no longer live
twilight zones
of anxious states of coma

I've had it
up to my third eye
with being what another needs me to be

I've had it
with men supporting hurricane I.Q.'s
and with their Judeo-Freudian mentalities
diagnosed as
"terminal female comprehension dysfunction"

I've had it
with being a pain junkie
and helping myself
to a slice of perhaps.

Oh Lord
nourish us with apples
where healing is in loving
allowing multiple heart orgasms,
where—
as my son Dimitry said at age six—
"perfect is imperfect"
where every event is sacred
where in pale blue,
sparkler of my blue roses,
we sing
the everlasting beauty
that is You!

---

1. According to Yogic philosophy, the seven
   centers of spiritual energy in the human body

MEDITATION PIECE

After rain
a full moon
reflects my shadow
gliding silently
among the garbage
and sidewalk
landing in a puddle

I contemplate my solitary
puddle-shadow reflection

From nowhere a raindrop falls
and shatters my image

I hear myself laugh

DEAREST LORD

Dearest Lord
how I so sweetly
crave Your center in me
the same words
I once said to a man

how I so sweetly
crave Your center in me,
the sweet thirst
for the spark
the joy of Your love

nothing else counts
but Your light
and Your love
so gently
within

THE TIBETAN ENCOUNTER GROUP

Tonight
full moon
and my muses are yearning
and churning

tonight
full moon
of self unemployment
singing your sweetest
most sweetest name

bewildered with finding
whenever I see you
a part of my life I thought was lost ...

tonight full-moon-hicky-time
of alpha brain wave fanatics
the Tibetan encounter group...

full moon
matching of auras[1]
where "getting high" junkies
develop flowers
in their third chakras[2]

tonight
full moon
drowning in air and letting go
a beingness without symbols
Revelation at last!

---

1. The light field surrounding living matter

2. According to Yogic philosophy, the seven centers
of spiritual energy in the human body

WE ARE HERE JUST TO SERVE

Dearest God in Your love
my heart burns in light
in the love for us all
You ennoble our sight

Here we gather to love
and pray to deserve
in the gift of this world
we are here just to serve

WAITING FOR MY BUS

A disheveled homeless guy
sees a bible in my hand
"It's a bible," he screams,
"Shove it up your ass!"
Our eyes meet in chaos
paralyzed
I don't answer of course,
his green gaze burns with fear...
the bus has arrived
I wrestle with my fright and
clutch my bible harder,
it is then that I remember
I'm not my brother's keeper
I am my brother...
I attempt to smile
and hear the bus drive off.
He abruptly turns his back and walks away.

33 years have passed
and I still recognize those eyes.

AGAIN AND AGAIN

In my heart I celebrate
Your presence in my brain
Your blazing mighty flame
the burning of my aim

Give me Divine Passion when I pray!
It's Your fire that I crave
fulfill my mouth with Your Endless Name
how I crave to see You in my dream again...!

I close my eyes
direct my thoughts to You
feel Your love all over me again
and the burning of Your presence
            Father
        again and again

Jewish Poems

AMONG THE RUINS,
THE WILD FLOWERS GROW*

Arbeit macht frei,
"Work makes free"
inscribed on top of the gate
and Auschwitz opens its doors.

In a collective chill
to a rhythm of soft sobs,
we enter the gate of death
some of us holding hands
not daring to look at each other's face
we walk in
and hope to understand.

"If I must see, please God, hold my hand."
Hand in hand
we march on the train tracks
the beat of my pace confused with
the roar of human cattle trains
packed with children's terrorized hearts
we walk, God's hand still in mine,
just as He walked with those terrorized hearts
when they bartered with death,
for God is everywhere, so they say...

Acres and acres and acres
of nazi commerce—the business of death.
They had blueprints,
skilled electricians and engineers
who washed off the stench of burned flesh
and night after night sat for a warm meal
with their golden children of blue sight.

Why? I ask
with my fist against the sky.
Why?
and the wind gently answers
with a faint smell of singed flesh.
The path changes color as we walk
from gray—
oh God, whose ashes are we walking on?—
to dark red...
Is the blood rising from the ground?
We are walking on earth that God forgot.

Faraway, a voice with no face,
a tour guide speaks German,
for a moment
a raging agony collapses time
now and then become one
rendering God ineffectual.

Suddenly a woman's burning scream
rips the heat of the sun
and in that cry, we hear the six million.

Facing the ovens
Michael prays *El Male Rachamim*
the prayer "Oh God full of mercy,"—
and among the ruins
the landscape of corpses,
huddled together even in death,
reveals itself among the wild flowers
and golden grass.

Still wandering forlorn on earth that God forgot
we cross the gateway of hell
into dark barracks filled with homeless prayers
where Jews lay famished
one on top of another, month after month.

A ray of light
filters through a crack
stealing a piece of sky.

Someone runs out of the barrack to throw up outside

Names on the bricks, scratched with fingernails
reveal themselves through the dark—
Sonya, Esther, Golde...—
and inside my head I hear myself scream
Grandma, where is your name?!

Drowned in holocaust
we turn to return

Our safe bus is waiting for us ...
Amiram picks up and clutches a stone
shedding tears through the sweat in his hand.
How can we leave?
Beloved ones, how can we leave you here?!
And the birds perched on the entrance door
where Arbeit Macht Frei
continue singing

---

* To the Holy Memory of my Grandparents,
  whom I never knew:
    Abraham and Zelda Klenburg
    Abraham and Haia Zelenietz

**To Rabbi Shlomo Carlebach, whose genius
brought us on a music pilgrimage to Poland

PILGRIMAGE*

Hungry for Jewish geography
with needs that time does not forget
we are filled with longing
Grandparents we never knew, cousins,
old blood thrusting to our hearts.

The "Singing Rabbi" with his guitar
leads us on tour
through this land of ancestry
in joyous alchemy.

The second concert
Leningrad
three thousand Jews awaken to their song
even the chairs sing!
Suddenly in the audience
one cigarette lighter flames
then ten, twenty
one hundred sunbursts in the night.

From city to city
the pilgrimage goes on
from tomb to tomb of holy sage
we feed on the holiness
held onto through 2,000 years of exile
bereft of our own country

    Babi Yar[1]
our longing for roots
confronted with Jewish massacre
eighty thousand Jews killed
again
    Babi Yar
filled with corpses, its river dried out
sobbing from dusk to dawn.

With holy hearts
drenched in hope
we wandering Jews
roam for families lost
in faraway villages
      Ladizchino, Berdichev,
      Dubki, Tarasha ...
returning with only a brick
from where the synagogue once was,
or a stone from the cemetery
that is no more.

Reb Shlomo
desperate with genius
a possessed earthly angel
gave Soviet brethren
with joy of awakening
the remembrance of
who they are.

---

*To the holy memory of my Rabbi
 Reb[2] Shlomo Carlebach

---

1 A gully in the Ukraine which became a mass
grave for Jewish nazi victims.

2 Respectful endearment for Master

HASHEM[1]

I wandered in
an autumn meadow
lamenting the absence of soulmate
I looked up at the sky
fell to my knees
and found The Beloved within

---

1. Literally means "The Name" and is used in
Hebrew to refer to God

REPRESSION, DEPRESSION, CONFESSION...

I look in the mirror
and see no image:
a stream of thoughtlessness
spilling itself into space.
Depression: perennial checkmate
Kadesh[1] of purposeless dream

Mythology of hope
reality of no hope.
God is gone once again,
I'm fed up and I sing
(of course out of tune)

Depression, repression, confession
Oh! It's useless to talk to The Wall [2]...

---

1. The Jewish mourners prayer.

2. The Wailing Wall in Jerusalem. The Holiest
site of Jewish worship

Three Early Poems in Spanish

ESCRITO EL DIA QUE CUMPLI 16

Te hundias y reias
tus navíos de amor dentro de mis oidos
máscara ya vivida.
Y mirando las oscuridades
nos vamos hacia dentro
enjambres de murciélagos.

Quien se ata por los silencios?
Tú, cerrado como boca hambrienta en verano
verano solitario y neurótico
lejanías, muros grises.

Estoy atada
a tu cuerpo de rio precipitado
precipitaciones de fulgores lunares
lluvia de meteoros en azoteas solitarias...

Pero nada de esto en realidad pasó.
Anoche me fui a dormir con 9 muñecas.

WRITTEN ON MY 16TH BIRTHDAY

You were sinking and laughing
vessels of love inside my ears
living a mask already lived.
Peering into a darkness
we're going towards the beyond within
swarms of bats.

Who is bound by silence?
You are closed like a starving mouth in summer.
Summer of distances and grey walls,
lonely and neurotic.

I am seized by
your body of rushing river
silent thunder of splendid moon
meteor showers on deserted roofs.

But none of this ever happened.
Last night I went to sleep with 9 dolls.

Translated from the Spanish
By Bob Boss in 1970

ESCRITO A LOS 18 AÑOS

Quiero pasar más allá de mí misma
y abrir una grieta en los montes,
he de llegar más profundo
que el agua de la lluvia
a la palpitación de la tierra.
Quiero cantar por tu sangre y la mía
y ver más allá
de las tinieblas verdes del trigo
y más allá de las estaciones.
Quiero arrancarme las entrañas
que en la fiesta de la noche se enmohecen,
girar y girar
como sus pensamientos hermanas y hermanos,
y abrazar en los crepúsculos
tus noches de miedos volcánicos
y hundirme los ojos
y fundir mis rodillas
y cercenarme mi centro

Me niego a comer mansamente en lo podrido

Saben mis compañeros humanos?
Esta tarde descubrí
que las hojas en los árboles
tienen dos colores,
y mis amigos tienen miedo
y los amigos de mis amigos
y sus vecinos
y las hojas de sus árboles
también tienen dos colores.
Cuanto dolor en sus hojas
en sus colores
en sus zapatos y en sus faldas;

WRITTEN AT AGE 18

I want to go beyond myself
and open a crevice in a mountain,
I've got to go deeper than rainwater
into the throb of the earth.
I want to sing through your blood and mine
and see beyond
the nebulous green of wheat
and beyond the seasons.
I want to uproot my entrails
that in the night's feast rust,
to whirl and whirl
as your thoughts, my sisters and brothers,
to join in your twilight of volcanic fear
and sink my eyes
and smelt my knees
and sever my center.

I refuse to tamely eat among what's rotten

You know, my fellow humans,
this afternoon I discovered
that the leaves on the trees have two colors
and my friends have fear
and my friends' friends
and their neighbors and their tree leaves
are bi-colored too.
Such pain in their leaves
in their colors
in their shoes and their skirts.

Tu dolor hermano
no es mayor
porque yo lo haya conocido.
Tanto dolor hermana
tanto dolor
que el mismo dolor se dolería.

Quiero pasar mas allá de mí misma
y unir nuestros dolores
y unir nuestros pesares
y unir nuestros ideales
y juntos hermana - hermano
lucharemos
para llegar libres
a vivir
a crear
y a cantar!

Your pain, brother-sister, is not bigger
because I have known it,
such pain that pain itself would hurt.

I want to cross beyond myself
and unite our pain
and unite our grief
and unite our ideals
and together, sister-brother,
fight to be free
to live
to create
and to sing!

ESCRITO A LOS 21 AÑOS

Ni antes ni después
de tu ternura, nadie
me acarició con tu alcance

Piel que a borbotones
canta su alegría

Mago de las mil y una estrellas
siembra tu nuca florida
en mi vientre de olores nocturnos
y amordaza el vacío sin fin
de mis horas

WRITTEN AT AGE 21

Not before or after
your tenderness, no one
caressed me with your reach

Bubbling over skin
singing its happiness

Magician of the thousand and one stars
plow your blooming nape
into my belly of nocturnal scents
and gag the endless emptiness
of my hours

and etcetera...

OH WHAT A DRAG!

Early morning:
yes, we all go alien
you know?
Doing nothing new to our shadows
we have not done to our selves.

Nightmares
daymares—

So I went for open
mind surgery
but my feet divorced me
on the way there.
The surgeon
of tequila persuasion
waited in vain.

Late morning:
looking at nothing
struggled with guts full of
chocolate-covered butterflies
spaced out in panicked ozone;
said never mind
in my mind
to God.

Life is a drag, you see
so tired today,
I can't remember
my own zodiac sign.

Desk piled with
patient patients' insurance forms
what is Mary Magdalen's social security number?!

What can I say?
I know God loves me...
He's just not ready
for a heavy commitment.

We're heading for a collective breakdown,

~

~

~

poetic interruptus
not fair
let's have an affair
yes!
in the rocking chair.

Afternoon:
left consciousness in bathtub
flooded my bedroom garden with tears
looked out the window
saw neighbor with soundproof toupee.

It's hard being a visionary.

Eve (as in night)
lay around like lox on a bagel
night table clock made silence loud;
played out my myths
and was betrayed by those myths
Hollywood's treason!
Came to the conclusion
the only thing left
was to teach courses on:
"How to be a goddess".

Most men are predictable
life is a drag
just is.

In short:
I have a pocket of air in my brain,
that's what I wanted to say from the start.
And no,
I'm not neurotic
I'm just catching a cold.

DISCOVERY

The noise that
  hunted my years and scared
  my sleepless nights was
  my heart's own beat.

MARTHA

She is 6
    and letting her father win at board games
    so he won't feel hurt
She is 8
    and her mother just died
She is 13
    and became her daddy's wife
    in more than one way
She is 17
    and on her record
    an entry of a second suicide attempt
She is 19
    and just got herself acquitted
    for stabbing her father in self-defense
She is 24
    and in and out of jobs
    and failed love affairs—
    deeply melancholic
She is 27
    and still in and out of jobs—
    dangerously depressed
She is 29
    and, as my patient, enters therapy
    for the first time doing for herself
She is 30
    still drowsy in anesthesia she mumbles:
    "my breast to cancer
    rather than to you. You were
    and still are the prick of the world."
She is 39
    finally resting her soul
    enveloped in softness
    married to the beloved of her heart
    her baby due in the spring,
    David will be his name
    and not William
    after her dead father
    as she heard he requested
    with his fruitless last breath.

LIKE HER NAME SHOULD BE ANNA

She entered the party like a walking bacchanal[1]
looking like her name should be Anna,
defying all logic, bumping auras[2] with the guys
she launched herself kamikaze[3]-fashion

Provoking the gods
Anna thrust us—mortals of the flesh—
into The Last Judgment

In stream of unconsciousness I scan the room:
"M ...m...m... She's giving good now ...
m...m... I wonder how Peter" (a devout bachelor)
"will react to her..."
(as I see his libido doing the lambada with Lori)
"She must be an anorexia worshiper ...
does she cry to her cafe au lait in the morning?"

Why judge and waste time, if life
is a sexually transmitted happening
with a fatal prognosis?

Realizing that this vehicle called Anna
was a karmic[4] overlap
I settled for Nirvana[5] nervosa—oh, not to judge!—
went onto the balcony facing the ocean
and decided to levitate

---

1. A participant in the ancient Roman festival in
honor of Baccus the god of wine. An orgy.

2.The light field surrounding living matter.

3.Japanese pilot trained to make a suicidal crash attack.

4.Karma: the law of cause and effect regarding
our actions in life and past lives according to Hindu
and Buddhist belief.

5. The state of absolute blessedness in Buddhism.
Nirvana Nervosa: a poetic play on words com-
bining Nirvana and anorexia nervosa.

ABOUT THE AUTHOR

Jana L. Klenburg was born in Mexico City and spoke Spanish and Yiddish for the first 20 years of her life. She earned a Masters Degree at Mexico's National University in drama and became a multiple award winning actress, performing in movies, her own TV programs, and leading roles in the theatre-classical, avant-garde, and soap operas. She has given many poetry readings, since age 17, and continues to this day.

Jana learned English at age 20 and moved to New York City at age 27, where she appeared in four Off-Broadway plays, Shakespeare in the Park, and as a star in a CBS-TV soap opera for a number of seasons. She has written poetry exclusively in English, since she moved to the United States.

She holds a PhD in psychology, has a thriving private practice in New York City, and leads numerous workshops and lectures widely. She has served on the faculty at the New Seminary and The American Psychotherapy Seminar Center.

Jana has deepened her spirituality through Judaism, Eastern philosophies and Christian principles as well as being a devoted student-practitioner-teacher of "A Course in Miracles" for 21 years.

A potter, artist, and jewelry-maker, Jana's talents found no greater fulfillment than in her children, Illana and Dimitry, her "deepest and sweetest gift."

ORDER FORM

Timeless Resonance by Jana I. Klenburg.

Postal Orders to:

Global Book Productions
23 West 35th Street
New York, NY 10001

Please specify the number of copies you require.
Include your name, address, and telephone number.

Most major credit cards accepted via telephone
orders.

Call: 1-800-212-609-6890. Local calls: 212-695-5703
Price per copy: $12.00 plus Shipping & Handling fee
($2.00). for total cost of $14.00.

New York State residents, please add $1.00 sales tax
(8.25%), for total cost of $15.00.

Poetry readings available upon request.